21st Century Skills Library

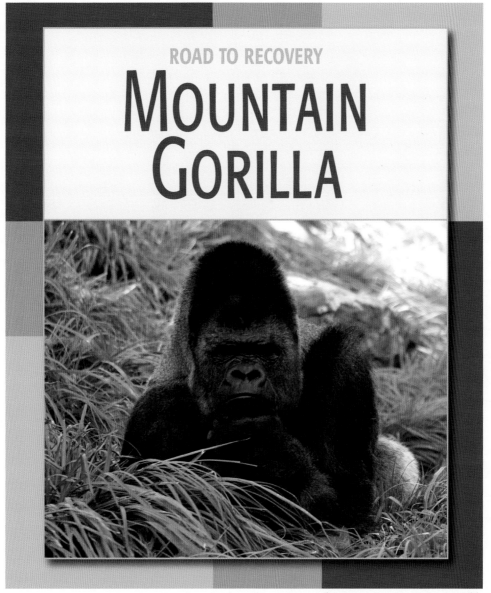

ROAD TO RECOVERY

MOUNTAIN GORILLA

Barbara A. Somervill

Cherry Lake Publishing
Ann Arbor, Michigan

Published in the United States of America by Cherry Lake Publishing
Ann Arbor, MI
www.cherrylakepublishing.com

Content Adviser: H. Dieter Steklis, Professor Emeritus of Primatology, Rutgers University, The State University of New Jersey, New Jersey

Photo Credits: Page 4, © Karl Ammann/Corbis; pages 6 and 21, © Martin Harvey; Gallo Images/Corbis; page 23, © Yann Arthus-Bertrand/Corbis; page 25, © Martin Harvey/Corbis; page 27, © Joe McDonald/Corbis

Map by XNR Productions Inc.

Library of Congress Cataloging-in-Publication Data
Somervill, Barbara A.
  Mountain gorilla / by Barbara A. Somervill.
    p. cm. — (The road to recovery)
  Includes bibliographical references and index.
  ISBN-13: 978-1-60279-033-9 (hardcover: alk. paper)
  ISBN-10: 1-60279-033-7 (hardcover: alk. paper)
  1. Gorilla—Juvenile literature. I. Title.
QL737.P96S588 2008
599.884—dc22   2007004601

*Cherry Lake Publishing would like to acknowledge the work of
The Partnership for 21st Century Skills.
Please visit* www.21stcenturyskills.org *for more information.*

TABLE OF CONTENTS

CHAPTER ONE

THE SILVERBACK BOSS

A silverback mountain gorilla bares his teeth to frighten away other animals.

A roar echoes through the mists. An unfamiliar male gorilla has appeared on the edge of the nesting site of a gorilla troop. The troop leader, called the silverback, loudly warns him away. The silverback pounds his chest, shows his teeth, and charges. Wisely, the other gorilla turns and disappears into the underbrush.

The troop is the name for a gorilla's group. It consists of the silverback, a younger adult male, several females, and their young. Without question, the silverback is the boss. At 22 years of age, he is at the peak of his power. The troop goes where he says, eats when he says, and sleeps when he sleeps. He leads; they follow. During rest or feeding, the juveniles clamber into his lap or on his back. If their behavior gets a bit wild, he disciplines them with a look.

Two troop females have young babies. While many animal infants quickly become independent of their mothers, this is not true for gorillas. A gorilla mother nurses her baby for nearly three years. The

Dian Fossey was a researcher who used her creativity and innovation skills to learn about mountain gorilla behavior. "I finally had the chance to put a mirror in front of one young adult's face!!!" she wrote. "He preened like a teenager getting ready for a prom—twisting his head from side to side with rather pursed lips . . . toward the end of that time [he] reached behind [the mirror] twice to feel for the animal that wasn't there."

oldest female in this troop is 18, and this is her third baby. Her infant clings tightly to her body during nursing and travel. For the first three years of its life, the baby will sleep with its mother each night.

Nearby, a five-year-old, considered a juvenile, yanks thistles out of the ground and feeds. Most gorillas prefer bamboo, but they eat where the

A mountain gorilla cares for her baby.

silverback says to eat. So today's menu is thistle.

Tomorrow may be gallium vine or wild celery.

By midafternoon, the troop has eaten, napped, and eaten again. Another nap and two more hours of feeding round out the day's activities.

As the sun sets, the silverback selects the overnight nesting site. He plops down in the middle of some tree leaves and folds the branches under his body. Within three minutes, his nest is built, and he settles down for the evening. Younger gorillas climb into trees and build sleeping platforms from twigs and branches.

CHAPTER TWO

THE STORY OF MOUNTAIN GORILLAS

Mountain gorillas are genetically related to humans. They can even frown like humans!

Ninety-eight percent of the genetic material in humans is also in gorillas. Great apes—chimpanzees, orangutans, and gorillas—are our closest relatives. They frown, laugh, and show anger. They play, learn, and use tools. They love their children and protect them from harm.

Gorillas have large, powerful bodies, but they are peaceful, gentle, and shy. The average silverback gorilla has an arm span of 6.6 to 9 feet (2 to 2.7 meters). Fully grown mountain gorilla males stand about 5.7 feet (1.7 m) tall and weigh roughly 440 pounds (200 kilograms). Females weigh about half as much and stand barely 5 feet (1.5 m) tall.

Mountain gorillas have black hair that is longer than other gorilla species. Both sexes have a high, bony crest on their heads, but the male's crest is more obvious.

Gorilla legs appear short and bowlegged. Arms are much longer and used for moving. Gorillas curl their hands and lean on their outer knuckles as they walk. This is called knuckle-walking. They have rounded bellies, and males have backs that seem to sag. Adult males develop a silvery-gray saddle of hair on their backs, which gives them the name silverback.

Plants of all kinds are the mountain gorilla's main diet.

Typical gorilla habitat is open forest with a great deal of undergrowth. This undergrowth is the gorilla supermarket. They feed on all sorts of plants, from woody bamboo to soft, blue-flowered lobelia. Wild celery and thistles are favorites. On occasion, gorillas also eat ants.

The basic diet is low in protein, so gorillas need plenty to eat. A hungry male might eat up to 60 pounds (27 kg) in a day, although about 45 pounds (20 kg) is more common.

In the Virunga volcanoes region, gorillas live in cloud forests up to 11,000 feet (3,353 m) above sea level. The air is cool, damp, and misty. Like humans, gorillas can have congested lungs. Wet, cold air can make the condition worse. Colds, coughs, and even pneumonia can sometimes lead to a gorilla's early death.

Gorillas live in troops that can have as many as 30, 40, or even 50 members. A troop may begin with just a lone female and a silverback looking for a mate. If the silverback is the king of the troop, the first female mate is the queen. Females may move from one troop to another several times during their lives. The males may dominate the troops, but the females choose their own mates based on their strength

and size.

Females reach adulthood at about seven or eight years old. At that

point, they leave their parents' troop to look for mates. Usually, females

will not have a baby until they are 10 years old. Males do not usually breed

until about 15 years old.

Pregnancy can occur at any time of the year and lasts for eight and a

half months. A female cannot have a new baby while nursing, so the time

between one birth and the next is about four years.

Gorilla infants cannot walk until they are three to six months old.

During the three years that they nurse, babies learn how to be gorillas.

They learn what to eat, how to behave, how to pick insects from fur, and

other important life skills.

A baby mountain gorilla feeds in a Uganda forest.

At three, a baby becomes a juvenile. Male and female juveniles are

extremely playful. They climb trees and build sleeping platforms above the

ground. They show affection for the silverback and wrestle each other.

All males want to mate, but it is usually a troop's silverback that fathers the young. Becoming the troop's silverback is a serious goal for male gorillas. A male may take over a troop from a sick or elderly silverback. A healthy male might challenge a silverback for his position and win.

Males also leave their home troops to look for willing females and the opportunity to found their own families. His place in a troop is very important to the male gorilla.

CHAPTER THREE

ENDANGERED!

When he is angry, a male mountain gorilla is large and intimidating enough to scare off most aggressors.

Gorillas have no true enemies other than humans. Occasionally, a lion or leopard may come and take a young gorilla. But for the most part, a charging silverback— roaring, thumping its chest, and baring its teeth—is frightening enough to send hungry meat eaters looking elsewhere for a meal.

Even Bwindi Impenetrable National Park isn't protected from development. Here farmers grow tea on park land in Uganda.

Centuries ago, humans may have also been frightened by chest-pounding silverbacks. However, the inventions of wire traps and guns have given the edge to humans. Powerful arms and flashing teeth cannot compete with bullets.

The major threats to mountain gorillas include loss of habitat, poaching, and disease. Rwanda, Uganda, and the Democratic Republic of the Congo are large countries with many poor people. The people cut down trees for timber and for making charcoal. They use wood fires for cooking and heat. They clear the land on which gorillas live so that they can graze cattle or plant crops. Even in national parks, agriculture eats away at protected forests. Timber companies clear-cut huge swaths of forest for profit.

While these activities benefit humans, they mean loss of habitat for mountain gorillas. Fortunately,

21st Century Content

The IUCN-World Conservation Union determines the degree to which a species is at risk of extinction. Other members of the mountain gorilla family have been classified by the IUCN as reaching at-risk status. Cross River gorillas are critically endangered, eastern lowland gorillas are endangered, and western lowland gorillas are endangered in Nigeria and Guinea.

Poachers have taken mountain gorilla babies from the wild.

the National Park Service has been patrolling the mountain gorilla habitat.

Timber companies are no longer allowed to cut down trees in those

regions. Similarly, poachers are kept at bay.

Poaching has been a serious problem for many years. In the past, poachers sold mountain gorilla hands and heads to collectors for display. It is believed they also sold live baby gorillas as pets for private zoos.

Putting an end to poaching will be a challenge. The areas where poaching takes place are remote. A nation would need an army of rangers throughout the region to stop poachers. Luckily, there has been no poaching of mountain gorillas for trophy hands or heads for years. Even so, eastern lowland gorillas and western lowland gorillas are vulnerable to poaching.

Human diseases continue to threaten gorillas. Because gorillas are so much like humans, they can

Learning & Innovation Skills

Gorillas are, in effect, nature's gardeners. They move daily from one feeding spot to the next. They tear up plants, prune trees to make sleeping nests, and eat leaves and seeds. They digest the food and pass it as solid waste. The waste fertilizes the soil, and the seeds in the waste spread plants throughout their territories.

Gorillas forage in a new area each day. Their careful movements allow the forest plants to recover and thrive until the next time the troop visits the area. What do you think would happen to the plants without gorillas?

get human diseases. Unfortunately, they have no doctors or drugstores to help them fend off illness.

In recent years, more than 5,000 western lowland gorillas in western Africa contracted and died from Ebola virus. So far, no mountain gorillas have gotten Ebola, but the potential is there. One infected human in contact with a troop could mean the end of mountain gorillas.

A team of veterinarians is on call to treat gorillas with life-threatening illnesses, especially diseases spread by humans. The Virunga gorillas have gotten shots to protect them against measles. Ill gorillas are captured in the field for treatment.

To prevent the spread of human diseases, preserves limit human contact with wild gorillas. There is no point saving gorillas from poaching only to infect them with human diseases.

CHAPTER FOUR

THE ROAD TO RECOVERY

A mountain gorilla's eyes look similar to a human's eyes.

"No one who looks into a gorilla's eyes—intelligent, gentle,

vulnerable—can remain unchanged, for the gap between ape and human

vanishes; we know that the gorilla still lives within us. Do gorillas also

In 2005, Rwanda's president Paul Kagame and villagers met to name 30 rare mountain gorilla babies. The chosen names include Kunga (peacemaker), Izuba (sun), Isoni (shy), and Inkurwa (loved). "The naming ceremony reflects our culture. We do it in families in Rwanda when we name new babies," said Fidelle Ruzigandekwa, head of the Rwanda Wildlife Agency.

recognize this ancient connection?" asked gorilla researcher George Schaller. But it was Dian Fossey who later drew the world's attention to the endangered status of mountain gorillas.

In 1966, Fossey, an American scientist, began a 13-year research study into the lives of mountain gorillas. She founded Karisoke Research Center in Rwanda in 1967. Fossey's method was to sit quietly some distance from a group and watch them. She hoped in time the gorillas would accept her presence. In 1970, she experienced her first physical contact with gorillas when Peanuts, an outgoing male gorilla, touched her hand.

*This photograph of mountain gorilla expert Dian Fossey
was taken in 1985, the year she was killed in Rwanda.*

Fossey gave names to each gorilla, usually based on their appearance or

personality. Her favorite gorilla was Digit, a male who was later attacked and

killed by poachers. Fossey established the Digit Fund, now known as the

Dian Fossey Gorilla Fund International, and told Digit's story to the world.

Fossey's Digit became the poster child for funding gorilla survival programs.

The Mountain Gorilla Species Survival Plan is simple enough on paper, but it has been a challenge to carry out. The two main parts of the plan are protecting the mountain gorilla's natural habitat and educating the public.

Protecting the habitat has been difficult. The local people need land for farming and cattle. Educating the public means educating the rest of the world, too. It is hoped that education will reduce the market for gorillas and gorilla body parts. If there is nowhere to sell the product, poachers will not risk capturing gorillas.

Today, there is no captive breeding program for mountain gorillas in zoos. This is because there are no mountain gorillas in any zoos. The gorillas in today's zoos are usually western lowland gorillas. Captive breeding is always an option if needed to save the species.

CHAPTER FIVE

MOUNTAIN GORILLAS TODAY

Here a safari guide clears away a mountain gorilla trap set by poachers in Virunga National Park. These kinds of efforts help increase mountain gorilla numbers.

There is good news concerning mountain gorillas—and bad news. Gorilla numbers are increasing in Virunga and remaining stable in Bwindi. Three projects are active in Rwanda's Parc National des Volcans: Karisoke, the International Gorilla Conservation Program, and the Virunga Veterinary Centre. Scientists in these programs learn about gorillas and ways to preserve the species.

A healthy population of mountain gorillas can make money through tourism. Increased tourism brings in money for research as well as hotels, restaurants, and jobs. Rangers, preserved lands, campaigns against poaching, and public education cost money. If the gorillas can bring in enough money to make their survival profitable, then managing their survival will be easier.

Money is the draw for poaching as well. Poachers can earn a year's wages by selling one gorilla infant. It is difficult to convince people not to poach when they need to feed their families.

In the past, poachers would capture baby gorillas and slip over the border from Rwanda to Uganda or Congo. Today, the three nations are combining efforts to stop these poachers. Their efforts may not eliminate poaching completely, but even reducing it by half would be a step forward.

A group of mountain gorillas rests and feeds in Rwanda's Parc National des Volcans.

Scientists understand that human contact with gorillas can be disastrous. The problems with Ebola virus and western lowland gorillas have conservationists concerned. "If chimpanzees and gorillas are in trouble in Gabon, an area known for its pristine, unbroken forests, then we have a

Life & Career Skills

Dian Fossey gave her life in her efforts to save mountain gorillas from extinction. Today, the organization that bears her name dedicates itself to research, conservation, and protection of mountain gorillas. The Dian Fossey Gorilla Fund International's Karisoke Research Center, established by Fossey in 1967, studies the animals and their habitats. The center also educates people about gorillas and works to prevent gorilla poaching. Fossey's organization is taking the lead to protect our wildlife. Setting high standards is the first step to reaching an important goal.

species-wide crisis on our hands," says Lee White of the Wildlife Conservation Society. Since there are only 700 mountain gorillas in existence, any outbreak of disease could result in extinction.

Gorilla populations grow very slowly, and there is no way to speed up the process. A female can only have one baby every four years. Slow as it might be, the population in Virunga is growing.

A recent count shows an increase of 17 percent since 1989. Is this increase enough for the species to survive? Both survival and extinction depend on humans. If we leave these peaceful creatures alone, gorillas might just thrive on their own.

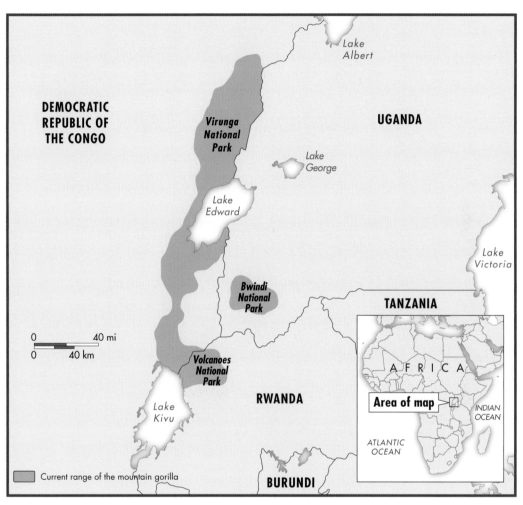

This map shows where mountain gorillas live in Africa.

GLOSSARY

captive breeding (KAP-tihv BREE-ding) a program to produce young in zoos or reserves

conservationists (kon-sur-VAY-shun-ists) people who work to preserve environments, animals, or plants

extinction (ek-STINGKT-shun) the condition of being extinct, or dying out completely

genetic (jih-NEH-tik) involving the characteristics passed from parents to their young through genes

habitat (HAB-ih-tat) the place where an animal or plant naturally lives and grows

juveniles (JOO-vuh-nilez) the young of a species

pneumonia (nuh-MOH-nyuh) an illness that affects lungs and makes breathing difficult

poaching (POHCH-ing) hunting game or catching fish in an illegal way

silverback (SIL-vur-BAK) the mature male gorilla who leads a troop

species (SPEE-sheez) a group of similar animals or plants

troop (TROOP) a group of gorillas

FOR MORE INFORMATION

Books

Ebersole, Rene. *Gorilla Mountain: The Story of Wildlife Biologist Amy Vedder.* Danbury, CT: Franklin Watts, 2005.

Nadin, Corinne. *Dian Fossey: Home with Mountain Gorillas.* Brookfield, CT: Millbrook Press, 2002.

Taylor, Marianne. *Mountain Gorilla: In Danger of Extinction!* Chicago: Heinemann, 2004.

Turner, Pamela S. *Gorilla Doctors: Saving Endangered Great Apes.* Boston: Houghton Mifflin Co., 2005.

Web Sites

Dian Fossey Gorilla Fund International
www.gorillafund.org
For more information about Fossey's organization

Mountain Gorillas
www.seaworld.org/animal-info/info-books/gorilla/index.htm
To see photographs of and read more about the mountain gorilla

World Wildlife Fund: Mountain Gorillas
worldwildlife.org/gorillas/subspecies/mountain.cfm
For a timeline showing the history of the mountain gorilla

INDEX

ABOUT THE AUTHOR

Barbara A. Somervill writes children's nonfiction books on a variety of topics. She is particularly interested in nature and foreign countries. Somervill believes that researching new and different topics makes writing every book an adventure. When she is not writing, Somervill is an avid reader and plays bridge.